Translating Love

Nikki Hart

BookLeaf Publishing

India | USA | UK

Presentation by *BookLeaf Publishing*

Web: www.bookleafpub.com

E-mail: info@bookleafpub.com

ISBN: 9789363300583

First edition 2024

For Kai, Sasha & Gemma:

It is not your responsibility to transform me, but it is my greatest honor and privilege to transform because of – and for - you. May my immeasurable, infinite, intense love for you always translate clearly.

For My Mom & Dad:

It is never too late to translate love, to translate happiness. I love you.

ACKNOWLEDGEMENT

To anyone who has ever read one of my poems, love letters, or handwritten cards, thank you for humoring me and giving me reason and inspiration to write. If I listed those who provided me positive feedback, I might be embarrassed by how sharp my bad memory is for long ago compliments (but trust me, I remember).

More recently, I am immensely grateful for Kate Stillman, Tatiana Mattos, Anita Avalos, Patricia Candido, and Nasrine Maktabi for reading poems and short stories on short notice, with open hearts, and providing me such helpful feedback and encouragement – some of them seeing my words more than they have seen my face (despite my lack of hesitation to share a good selfie).

To Walter Woods, thank you for your beautiful words in response to Safe Love (Joshua Tree), unknowingly gifting me my title poem, well after my heart was wed to the collection title.

I am beyond grateful to Beyond Baroque Literary Arts, both for my first poetry workshop and introduction to an amazing, brilliant writers' group; Village Well (Culver City) for giving me a place to write when I needed peace, energy and a great brownie; Veda Yoga and Jillian Modes for helping me clear space in my head and heart; Stacie Aamon, who helped me find the path to my higher self and held my hand in the rockiest parts of the journey; and Sylvie Targhetta for giving my energy a voice and giving me validation, for telling me to write instead of worry.

To Tulum, Mexico and Marciano, Italy: my trips to you this year gifted me beauty, magic, majesty; a richness from which I will never look back.

To my Brooklyn Mommas – Miriam Milord, Sherri McGee, Chamin Ajjan, Heather Romero and Vanessa Rodriguez – you inspire me; thanks for always having my back. To Derek Matthews, you've encouraged me to write many times over 27 years, thank you.

To Athletes Unlimited, for being an oasis and shining example of integrity, support and professional love. For David Glass and everyone at EPGR Lawyers for embracing me without question or pause.

Pra Leticia Castro, por ser uma alma amorosa, uma amiga gentil e familia. Por tudo que se tornou familia pra minha alma e coraçao quando aprendi português e compartilhei um sobrenome - Caldeira - que me transformou nesta vida: fico grata e com amor, pra sempre. Seus espaços em meu coração, permanente. Urso, saiba que existem lindas palavras indescritíveis de amor e crescimento tecidas neste apelido.

To Kai, Sasha & Gemma, thank you for being my beautiful People; I will forever search for words that do justice to how deeply and completely I love you. To my Mom, Dad and sister Billi, thank you for being my original professors of both love and language.

To those I will soon get the chance to love and be loved by, I am now better prepared.

PREFACE

"All language is but a poor translation." ~ Franz Kafka

"A real love letter is made of insight, understanding, and compassion. Otherwise it's not a love letter. A true love letter can produce a transformation in the other person, and therefore in the world. But before it produces a transformation in the other person, it has to produce a transformation within us. Some letters may take the whole of our lifetime to write." ~ Thich Nhat Hanh

*****

Within this collection, most words that aren't in English are Portuguese (Brazilian), with five poems translated completely into Portuguese. This country, culture, and language has been a professor of love for me, even before my feet stepped on Brazilian sand this lifetime.

All translations are at my own novice hands, so no doubt a little more poetic in their clumsiness. Todas as traduções foram feitas por minhas mãos novatas, portanto, sem dúvida, um pouco mais poéticas na sua falta de jeito.

There is one meaningfully placed Italian word in the poem "Slowly". The poem "Temenos (Translating Love)" is built around the Greek word and concept within the title.

Table of Contents

Safe Love (Joshua Tree)

i wondered
how the dry air,
brown dirt, tumbleweeds
of joshua tree could soften this
stone overtaking my heart. but then
the rough ground welcomed the salt of my first
tear,
born not yesterday, not near any ocean, but in
the dry summer
air of another prairie town, when my exposed
ankles with ruffled socks

collected countless stickers, the wind pushing
around tumbleweeds so carelessly.

the land thirst
for the water falling
from my eyes, born in
quiet cul-de-sacs of a small
town where I learned love was
many things, but not safe. the dry
shrubs, crackling and bristling in the heat,
understood the danger of fire, a lesson my bare
little thick legs learned as they pressed against
the
brick forming a fireplace, with a gun pointed at
my head.
the danger i learned in the backyard alcoves
formed by similar
fireplace bricks and tall wooden fences, when
my innocent shouts
of no were disregarded, mocked by teenagers
who lived on quiet streets,
my memory of how i found myself unscathed in
my own bed forever inaccessible.

the dirt opened
and softened for my
tears, born when i was
gifted shame for moving and
twisting my body the way i enjoyed

by the same middle age mouths that had
drool dripping from their corners. this earth did
not reject the flow of tears, trapped inside me so
long
ago when the very men who were quick to note
the extra flesh
protecting the bones of eight-year-old legs glued
their eyes to the
same flesh they criticized, ensuring that my soul
carried the guilt of their thoughts.

this land
underneath my
feet in joshua tree
knew i sought refuge
in the same water filling
countless backyard pools and
hot tubs, where a body could hide
from heat and glares and quiet danger
under the ripples of the surface. but my
grace in the captured water allowed those
without the need for protection to forget i was
just 8, just 9, just 11, just a girl and at the same
time remember that, with my two defenseless x
chromosomes,
I could be the one held accountable for their
thoughts and indiscretions.
water, in its transparency, is no good refuge
when you need to breath air.

the dry air
cradled me, as
i lay in the hammock
feeling the fear of teenage
boys guarded by unlocked doors
and empty streets whispering words
of indecency while they licked their lips,
feeling the fear of silence when there should
be noise, of screams when there should be
silence.
feeling the fear of a little girl collecting stories
of love
in which the adjective "safe" could not be
written except
for to note, with desert clarity, its stark and
devastating absence.

the prickling
cactus and joshua
trees offered empathy
as i avoided their touch,
understanding that there is
no other way to protect yourself
except with pinching thorns that grow
outward from your heart when you are tasked
with being so nice and so good and so perfect so
as

to compensate for the sins of others, sins which
you can't
name or know but you can identify by the
tightness that crawls
from your fingertips up your arms, across your
chest and closes your throat.

the desert knows
my addiction to love
that lacks safety and does
not shout or condemn me as
i realize the danger embedded in
the footprints across my mind make
the very thing that i name love the exact
opposite, and somewhere along my timeline i
directed
that opposite of love onto this six-year-old
housed inside me.

no, it does
not shout, it does
not scream, it does
not criticize or mock or
glare. no judgment exists in the dust
littered with prickly slivers born from the
strength of the unguarded sun. the heated brown
ground absorbs my tears and somehow
transforms the

perseverant succulents into beauty, into art
forms, into magical
statues of transformation that makes moisture
seem abundant despite its lack.

please transform me.

with each
sprinkle of salt
water around my bare
feet, a star appears in the dark,
black, deep, neverending sky. as if
to remind me that energy can be transformed.
earth to sky. dust to light. finite to infinite. stars
are not stagnant and I can see them move most
brilliantly
in the darkest nights and that is where the safest
love might be found.

just look in, just look in, just look up, just look
up. you're already transformed.

Riding Horses Backwards
(Co-Dependency)

Didn't I mention? I am expert at riding on horses
backwards.
I mean, it petrifies me, but you will never know
this.
It hurts my back, to face the opposite way the
horse is moving,
having to grip the horse's side muscles with my
legs arching
behind me in such an awkward way,
to be pushed toward the tail and
further from the protection of the horse's neck,

a neck kept sacred for the first rider (you).
But I don't complain.

You like to have company while the horse loses
control, right?
Choose me: I am expert.

I am so good at trying to grab
the reigns you are supposed to be holding,
the ones you released long ago, laughing in the
wind,
your hands up high over the horse's head.
The horse will go wild, and I will be slipping off
the right side of the horse,
but leaning so far to the left to try to grab that
reign
that will fall near your foot.
Gravity and the jolt of the horse might pull me
down -
at least, might cause the top of my head to
scrape the ground.
But I know, just in the nick of time and with just
sufficient energy,
no more,
you will grab foot,
Save me.

Really, don't worry about me.
I am expert at this.

My bruises can be hidden, the scrapes heal fast.

The horse will feel panicked with all its
freedom-
not having direction, neither of us knowing what
it is doing.
Your laughter will spike each time the horse
kicks itself high,
which will make me cry, but don't worry:
you will only see my back, not my tears.
People will run away from the wild horse
with us on it, facing backwards,
the horse out of control,
but one of us will appear to have control (you, of
me).
They will think the wind is making my eyes
water.

Really, I am expert at all of this.
No one will know it is one of us,
which one of us?, causing my tears,
or that I am as scared of the wild horse
as they are.

I'll be worried as I sense the horse move with
reckless abandon toward people you might love,
but that I cannot see or keep safe.
I'll do my best to stay on the horse and grab the
reigns

that have fallen to the ground and can't be seen
amidst the
cloud of dust this horse (not you, not me) is
causing.
But this cloud of chaos will hide my worry,
even if my eyes
betray me.

A near impossible feat:
controlling a horse with reigns lost in dust as
thick as fog
from the frantic kicking of an uncontrolled –
near feral - horse,
facing backwards in front of
a man facing backwards
with his hands free to hold me
but for being raised in the air
to announce his own pleasure,
neither of us watching where the wild horse is
jolting.

But I am expert at impossible feats.

If you laugh, I will laugh.
If you scream in delight, I will scream
and you can pretend it is ecstasy.
You won't have to acknowledge
the tears falling down my cheeks:
the water caused

by the wind
or one of us
or that pit in the middle of my stomach
where the knowledge
(that I shouldn't be riding a horse backwards
with
a man riding a horse backwards with the reigns
of the horse dragging in the dust, tangling
around
the angry horse's feet,
people all around us)
sits, ticking with a disappearing fuse.

But your arms will be around me,
your hands clenched right
where that tangle of nerves feels like a bomb.
Never mind that scent of amber and rose on your
palms,
I'll convince myself the horse's mane is made of
roses,
the tail brushed with amber oil,
scents that should calm me.
Because you'll be keeping me safe, right?,
as safe as you are keeping yourself.

And you really are expert at riding horses
backwards:
never, in fact, have you ridden one forward.

Please, don't worry about all these vulnerable
people
right in this angry, kicking, wild horse's path:
I'm expert at using all my will to control things
entirely out of my control
so that men can do things like
    ride horses backwards,
    drive motorcycles blindfolded,
    jump off the wrong end of diving boards,
    play with loaded guns,
    sleep through jobs,
    stand on top of moving cars,
    drink liters of vodka,
    turn steering wheels with blurry vision,
    crash cars through living room walls,
    set fire to necessary fences,
    Hide
and continue to believe they are in control,
that they do not risk hurting any single person.

I mean, I like to hide, too.

With my most athletic maneuvers to gain control
of the horse –
and, trust me, I am an athlete, I am expert at
athletic maneuvers –
I'll help you hurt the least amount of people
possible.

Hurt no one, really, except Me,
as my arms, and ribs, and legs, and head, and
shoulders, and
heart
get ripped apart.
Don't worry, I will absorb
the full supply of fault for these injuries,
leaving no demands on you.

At this, I am expert.

When I finally fall from the horse,
landing on the cloud of dust
with open wounds and dress ripped off,
I'll move fast, fearing only the horse.
You'll be having so much fun on your
wild, bucking, angry horse,
that the vision of my scraped, naked skin
will be a blur,
a beautiful, violent
dream.
There won't even be time to stop and say
Goodbye,
let alone see my bloody skin and ripped tendons
and shredded muscles
or the water still dripping down my cheek
despite that the wind has stopped.
I mean, really, who needs a "goodbye" when
she's done something so tremendous

as ride on a horse backwards with you?
Certainly not me.

I am the expert at knowing that words aren't
available
from men who ride horses backwards.

Physics dictates that words would come out of
your mouth
but blow right by my ears, given the speed of the
crazy horse,
so the air and syllables would be
wasted.
I know this already.
Besides, what words could preserve your fun
and mend this beating organ in my chest
that has been torn to shreds?
None really.
No words that you know of:
Silence the obvious choice.

And I am expert in these obvious choices, don't
worry.

Even then, after my blood has dripped across the
battlefield
and I've been charged by my conscience
for wounds caused by the hooves of this horse

that I couldn't control despite how good I am at
controlling things
out of my control,
you'll be able to keep riding, untethered by guilt,
untethered by concern,
knowing that you rode with at least one person
truly expert
at riding horses backwards,
even if you can't
remember
(it was)
Me.

An Entire Story
(Uma História Inteira)

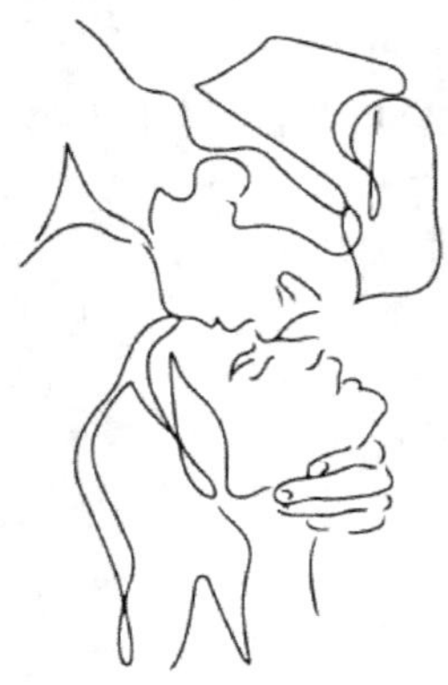

an entire story,
a lifetime,
between the time -

his thumbs gripped
right above the invitation
of her hipbones,
birthing a new rhythm
to his pulse;
the curves of her flesh -
perched on the very edge
of the wooden counter -
taught his palms how
to crawl, to pull, to guide, to sculpt,

with firm tenderness;
his fingerprints witnessed
the opposition of tan lines
and the subtle map of freckles,
absorbing their intricate detail,
the route never to be forgotten;
he grew as a man
when his gaze caught
the speckles of gold
that danced from her eyes;
he swallowed the taste of glistening *saudades*
with the light mist of her sweat,
surrendered to the medicine
that would extend his memory -

and his next inhale.

a perfect (life, love) story
told in the infinity
between
two breaths.

***

uma história inteira,
uma vida inteira,
entre o tempo

polegares dele agarrados
logo acima do convite

de quadris dela,
dando à luz um novo ritmo
ao seu pulso;
as curvas de sua carne -
empoleirado na beira
do balcão de madeira -
ensinou suas palmas como
rastejar, puxar, guiar, esculpir,
com firme ternura;
suas impressões digitais testemunharam
a oposição das linhas bronzeadas
e o mapa sutil de sardas,
absorvendo seus detalhes intrincados,
o percurso nunca será esquecido;
ele cresceu e se tornou um homem
quando seu olhar pegou
as manchas de ouro
que dançou em seus olhos;
ele engoliu o gosto de saudades brilhantes
com a leve névoa de seu suor,
rendendo-se ao remédio que estenderia
sua memória -

e próxima inspiração dele.

uma história perfeita (de vida, amor)
contado no infinito
entre
duas respirações.

Translate

how do I translate with
such damaged words
that have traveled the
unpaved road
from my chest to the
front of my mind,
only to be punished
and criticized by the
quiet chameleon who
calls herself my protector
but I secretly know
her name to be fear.
the letters of words
have been pulled apart
and reordered into
her logic yet sound like

nonsense to that piece
of me that birthed
what I am trying to explain.
how far back in time
do I need to travel
to find the hieroglyphics
that accurately decode and convey
this feeling in the
left side of my chest,
radiating out only far enough
to steal air from my lungs
and crowd my ribcage,
given that I have tried to convey
with words as weaponized as

love hate longing grief joy elation confusion
majestic homesickness
gratitude devastation loneliness terror beauty
and pain

but all have divinely failed.
how do I translate what feels like
the entire universe with
such wreckage of
words.

Hostages

The moment presents itself
with silence, a quick but
steady gaze.
I wonder: What are we trying to say?

Words form in my heart,
and shoot up to my mind.
Somehow, though, they skip my throat,
my tongue unable to find sound.

I can't give shape to the long sound of "I",
the soft click of "t",
the rolling moan of two "o"s,

the abruptness of the letter "k".

The word "want"
gets held back by the strong grip
of my soul, desperate to guard itself.
My desire to speak held hostage,
there's wounded certainty that silence is better
than being misunderstood,
or worse: being understood but deemed
undeserving.

What would happen
if I could push the words out
against my fear's strong will?
If the sounds born in my heart
were given permission and power
to travel to your ears, be translated for your
heart?

I took a shower
right before you arrived home
wanting a compliment,
"You look beautiful",
or, at least: to be seen.

I forgave you, gently and completely
for all that I was still unaware,
when I said, you in the shower, "Hi there",
with hopes you'd invite me to join,

that we could make love, to make peace,
that your lips would find my body,
act as eager erasers to my poorly hidden hurt.

I stayed out of the house all day,
hoping to rid it of my constant energy,
so that you might miss me, somehow,
despite that you can't be there,
a hostage to your responsibilities,
or, worse: to your escapes.

Last night I could not sleep
so I sat under the gaze
of the abundant tree with
over-trimmed branches on just one side,
making bare the side that greets us every day.
How can I avoid focusing on what is lacking,
how can I not hear the silence?

A light mist started at 3:45am,
the lightest touch of water, tender.
All alone, I realized the reason
the water on Réveillon felt so magic –
felt like floating on clouds of love,
generated straight from my own heart,
floating forward to more love.
Once quenched, my soul did not hold my truths
hostage,
all the words given freedom to run to you.

And you welcomed them with the embrace
of a lover weighted with longing,
reciprocating their honesty,
gifting your words to me.

How magical, talking;
even better: with truths.

Two hostages released.

Unabashedly

"my hand is missing something",
i would say,
letting my open hand dangle,
peacefully,
until it was filled with
such tiny warmth and force,
her clinging unabashedly
to be held.

"i want to lay with you,"
she would say,
climbing through the vacant side of my bed,
quietly,
until my body was met with
such tiny force and warmth,
her arms unabashedly thrown

around my neck.

"don't grow,"
i'd dream,
pushing each side of them
smaller,
as if they were boxes,
using such tender force and warmth,
me clinging unabashedly
to be in control.

"help me," he'd say; "i don't know how,"
i'd cry,
wiping the tears from his still tender face,
brokenly,
knowing he is no longer the little one,
roles reversed too soon,
yet he still turns to me,
almost unabashedly.

"come back to me,"
i mouthed,
reaching for the girl falling right in front of me,
desperately,
until my arm extended beyond
the black hole of the world,
returning empty-handed,
failing abashedly.

somewhere in between
all these moments
lies
the warmth of love
and force of loss.
and yet, still,
we love.

Little Lessons

the deal breaker, the guarantor of tragedy for me,
for you (for us):
alcohol overconsumed, the scent of nicotine,
invisible poisons dilating eyes.
these, I thought, the source of horrors to avoid (i
did) at all costs:
a foolish mirage of safety, until i (naively) and
you (with intent) did not.

such high functioning facades. now: true terrors
taught (by whom). a curriculum
of dark superficiality, drunk shapeshifting, heavy
vacancy, bitter betrayals.
the hungover moments with bitter "mentiras"
meant to mend truths
only to silently fall like gravity, unstoppable,
through our hands, consumed with foolish
"cafuné", and love.

you both, you three, you all: so big, so worthy
of blame. but it was my legs that were chiseled
with muscle,
having (endured and) perpetuated heavy crimes
while
i held you (accountable).
how do you, do i, (do we), do i apologize
to my selves. over and "de novo" and over. and
over.

Narrator

"if I could return in time,
i would do many things
differently."
when translated,
a dozen words of
an apology, arriving to my
heart, as fragile
as the shell that surrounds
a life still forming.

an inquiry into what would
be rewritten, if time travel and
wisdom allowed,
almost tumbled out
of the ancient bruises
of my heart,
deep purple and black from their
effort to find
those evasive stories

that align with (my) love
language.

the risk of
hearing which scenes
would be edited
stopped me:
i had known these scripts for too many lives,
even the (scenes)(lives) for which this body was
absent.
my desire: only the beautiful revision,
the final draft,
the yet unwritten.

i erased my question,
instead,
closing my eyes to
feel:
the safe embrace
of sunkissed water,
sparkling with the reflection
of a warm sunset,
the transcendent glitter of my soul;
the invitation of a reverential gaze,
consuming me,
from eyes still searching for their muse;
the sensation of being
        (w)holy,
a flutter not quite (un)known.

how unfair of me,
nearly handing him the task
of narrating a story
(that)(i) still needed to form.

Inside Games

you'd play
catch with my heart,
drums with my ribs.

these three
beings believed me
until they didn't.

you'd dance
tap on my lungs,
jazz around my bones.

these three
beings believed me
until they didn't.

you'd create
stories with my swallows,
paintings where I was hollow.

these three
beings believed me
until they didn't.

you'd hide
on my left side,
seek shelter on my right.

these three
beings believed me
until they didn't.

I can teach
you all the lessons,
lead you all the ways

these three
beings believed me
until i couldn't.

i can protect
you from the dark,
position you in light.

these three
beings believed me
until i couldn't.

i will fill
our home with joy,
our hearts with extra soothing.

these three
beings believed me
even when i didn't.

I will love you
when I don't know how,
when it seems -to you -
a distant reach,
outside of now.

these three
beings believe me.

Sweet Girl

how can I show you,
sweet girl,
how to get so caught up
in the act of being yourself
that it can't be called an act?

how can I convince you,
sweet girl,
that when you are absentmindedly
lost in your quirky ways
that you are exactly the opposite of absent?

how can I entice you,
sweet girl,

to keep open all those coverings
so wrongly eager to provide shadow,
when that seed of You needs sun?

how can I invite you,
sweet girl,
to talk not only to the mirror
and that fascinating mind,
but to the world at large, to the sometimes
not-so-kind?

how can I teach you,
sweet girl,
that when you move the way you move without
a thought of moving
that you move infinite hearts?

how can I prove to you,
sweet girl,
that when you appoint yourself
the perfect muse for your creations
a line will form, offering you that designation?

how can I demonstrate to you,
sweet girl,
that all those accents you want never to be heard
or seen
are the very imperfections
that will lead you to your dreams?

how can I show you,
sweet girl,
how to get so caught up
in the act of being yourself
that it can't be called an act?

but rather, right there,
right very there,
you are caught up
in your Beauty.

Slowly

always moving fast -
my feet, my thoughts, but not
my lungs or heart.

the desire, depth.
each moment filled with profound
layers. deceiving:

appearing steady,
if not calm, but lifetimes lived
thru growth, dusk to dawn.

maybe I was not
proceeding, but escaping
that both sought and feared.

now my steps' rhythm,
adagio: time to pronounce
each vowel, syllable

of a language
that translates to and for me
but only slowly.

Soft Sounds

our time together built
like sounds of an alphabet
tumbling together
to form words
we learned along the way,
with exceptions overpowering rules.

some days flowing with the
beauty of a soft consonant
lulling me into love.

unless the days were followed
by an event requiring
the closing of a mouth,
then, instead, becoming
all but forgotten:

the lost negatives of film.

some weeks sun poured
into us, our faces bronze with
the kiss of adventures,
until we leaned against
silence, as stark and present as a vowel,
without so much as a breath
transforming the sensation to hate.
and yet, still,
there, lived hours of miracles,
leisurely breaking all the rules
of past, future, and present tense,
seizing in me something that
was foreign but easy to give,
an ancient ingredient
in my veins.

the hardest days stood
identical,
not one difference to note.
the definite articles becoming indefinite,
the tense once again reversed.
those days, my only hope: to read.
looking for clues not to be found,
pretending i was already
the master
of the(se) sounds.

alone, caught off guard,
i was an island,
not understanding the reason
or value of my every letter.
existing maybe only to curve
to unknown desires
pronounced as if
announcing
the end.
like novice speakers,
we could not conjugate
what it was to love -
not correctly or at all.
so it all remained
aspirational,
theoretical,
an act undone,
never able
to be a
soft sound.

Subjects: My Muse
(Assuntos: Minha Musa)

"what do you write about?",
he asked.
words of

tears falling on a long
island railroad platform,
the colors of sunsets, the
scent of the NICU, the
trees in the West Village,
the space rage consumes as
it seeps through skin,

handwritten notes to
fairies, idiomas diferentes,
the awkwardness of a sound
that's never been made,
insufficiency of words,
memories of tumbleweeds,
freckles, the taste of a
half of a half under your
tongue, cobblestone streets,
knowing glances, chain link
fences, movement of bodies,
bruises, witnessing the last day
of a life, tightness in my chest,
the relief of honesty, sunlight,
crescent moons, unforgettable
voices, minnows,
fleeting moments,
miracles

all tumbled through my mind.
"love,"
i answered.

***

"sobre o que você escreve?",
ele perguntou.
palavras de

lágrimas caindo em um longo
plataforma da ferrovia de Long Island,
as cores do pôr do sol, o
cheiro da UTIN, o
árvores no West Village,
a raiva do espaço consome como
infiltra-se através da pele,
notas manuscritas para
fadas, different languages,
a estranheza de um som
isso nunca foi feito,
insuficiência de palavras,
memórias de ervas daninhas,
sardas, o gosto de um
metade da metade sob o seu
língua, ruas de paralelepípedos,
olhares conhecedores, elo da corrente
cercas, movimento de corpos,
hematomas, testemunhando o último dia
de uma vida, aperto no peito,
o alívio da honestidade, da luz solar,
luas crescentes, inesquecíveis
vozes, peixinhos,
momentos fugazes,
milagres

tudo passou pela minha mente.
"amor,"
eu respondi.

What Do You Call This?

When someone's presence hugs you, what do
you call this?
When it melts you, makes you forget your
resolve, lose your bearings.
What exactly is this?

When his presence feels like a first sip of wine.
Feels like a direct beam of sun on bare skin,
Feels like gently sinking into warm sand.
Feels like the a wish on a star, right when a wish
is nothing less than essential,
with a thousand more stars simultaneously
appearing so you can't quite tell which one you
wished upon.
Feels like the last step required to reach the most
beautiful vantage point,

makes you forget the word sad.
Feels like a smile, like an unbelievable view,
like a clean slate.
Feels like cold water slipping over your skin as
you dive under a wave,
taking your breath but making you stronger.
Feels like relief.

When his presence causes you shed a layer of
uncomfortable skin,
each time you see him,
bringing you closer to the best you,
the you that feels least censored,
most like You.
Feels like dejá vu
to something that hasn't happened in this
lifetime.
What do you call that?

What do you call this,
When you think of someone until you cannot
think of him anymore?
When you have two projectors in your mind, just
to open up space for other thoughts.
When you need to visualize not thinking of him
to make that a possibility.
What is this?
When there are words wrapped up and tangled
in his name.

Words you can't say separately, can't even
identify, but need to announce.
When your mind listens to him saying your
name, just to ensure you remember what your
name should sound like.
What is the name for this?
What exactly do you call this?

When you intimately know anger, and hurt, and
confusion, and regret, and disappointment, and
pain,
but it is something else that makes you cry?
When you feel the lump there in your heart
before it shatters your voice,
Feel it from the hairline where you begin to push
your hair behind your ear to the toe peeping out
of your shoes, fidgeting as you try to stay
composed and fail.
Feel your failure, tears falling from your eyes,
tinted with relief and worry and something that
has no tint.
When you try to connect, to capture, to vocalize
whatever this is to just one word.
What is the word?

What is it when you realize that the other
emotions - bigger in reputation - are mere
shadows to
Whatever this is you

Feel for him but should feel for you,
    if you could just find You.

What do you call it when your want is for his
content,
When your need is for his peace, even if you are
part of neither.
When you see him pushing a heavy stone up a
hill, and are willing to offer your strongest
muscle –
stronger than your shoulders, stronger than your
legs, stronger than the muscle that feeds blood to
all other muscles, that beats beautifully and
strongly and selflessly –
but somehow (miraculously, painfully) you
don't, because you can't,
    because you finally just found the shadow of
You.

What do you call this when you (almost) contain
this beating muscle that normally can't be
contained?
This feat feels (nearly) impossible.

I need to know what you call this.

Silence (Silêncio)

how big the quiet loomed over me
when i, so small, expected words.
the empty space would fill, inevitably,
with shadows of all the things to fear:

scarecrows as big and broad as men
making noise but lacking courage;
feet and legs once steady, now tumbling,
eyes darting back and forth, rummaging for
valuable hiding space;

kidnapping not kids, but the sounds
that could save us: music, laughter, screams;
drowning while the guard was on duty,
and, the worst, answering questions honestly.

what shock, then, to discover truth - fleeting,
almost pure -

looming safely over me, so grown, once silence
tumbled on us.

***

quão grande era o silêncio que pairava sobre
mim
quando eu, demais pequeno, esperava palavras.
o espaço vazio preencheria, inevitavelmente,
com sombras de todas as coisas a temer:

espantalhos tão grandes e largos quanto os
homens
fazendo barulho, mas sem coragem;
pés e pernas antes firmes, agora caindo,
olhos correndo de um lado para o outro,
procurando por um esconderijo valioso;

sequestrando não crianças, mas os sons
que poderiam nos salvar: música, risos, gritos;
afogando-se enquanto o guarda estava de
serviço,
e, o pior, respondendo honestamente às
perguntas.

que choque, então, descobrir a verdade - fugaz,
quase pura -
pairando com segurança sobre mim, tão
crescido, uma vez que o silêncio caiu sobre nós.

Ahem Prema

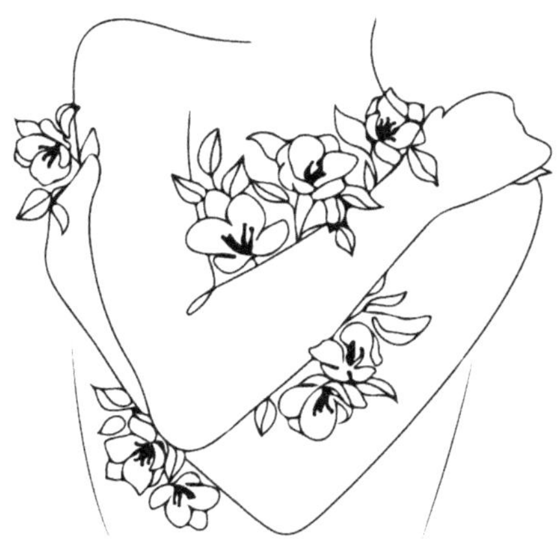

Eager to loosen my hips,
I learned pigeon pose,
Until the pose taught me
How to loosen my heart.

With a desire to chisel my thighs,
I practiced warrior flows,
Until the flows led me
To lay down my chiseled guard.

Aching to elongate my spine,
I stood firm in mountain,
Until the stance required me
To stand tall in my softening.

Yearning to release the tension in my shoulders,
I'd fold quickly into triangle,
Until the three points of the shape
Released in me something holy.

Longing to define my round curves,
I'd fiercely settle into utkatasana,
Until the chair supported
The weight of all my once fleeting joy and long
held grief.

Hoping to strengthen every corner of my
abdominal core,
I'd blossom into tree pose,
Until the roots brought to balance
A deeper core I'd previously ignored.

Impatient to realign my posture,
I'd push into cobra,
Until the upward curve of my body
Shed the scaly layer of inhibition around my
soul.

Yearning to create a sensual outline for my
entire body,
I'd settle into goddess pose,
Until I, surprised, greeted this goddess,
Not in my pose, but in the mirror, my essence,
my deeds.

Needing to shut out the world,
I'd collapse into shavasana,
Until right there, laying still,
I saw the entire world inside of me.

Eager to learn movement,
I arrived at class quietly,
Until, with beautiful loud breaths and gentle
humming lines,
I realized what I am learning is love, divine.

(in dedication & deep gratitude to Veda Yoga &
Jillian Modes)

Saudades (Saudades)

to pronounce it
correctly
there is space for
each vowel
as it floats from
your lips, tongue, mouth

the consonants
all soft
as if to embrace
the emptiness
as it overtakes
your heart, mind, soul

proceeded by
com*

followed by pra* or de*
but powerful enough
to stand alone
as it captures
your lungs, blood, dreams

the end and beginning
linger
as if to refuse
disappearance
long after
the word is complete

it persists, stays,
grows
as if to replace
the subject
who, for reasons unknowable,
has walked away

it lays soft in my
palm
as if to fill
the broken lifelines
pronounced
for having held too tight

after learning this
word

your being remains
with saudades*,
as if it's required
to live

***

pronunciá-lo
corretamente
há espaço para
cada vogal
enquanto flutua de
seus lábios, língua, boca

as consoantes
tudo macio
como se fosse abraçar
o vazio
à medida que ultrapassa
seu coração, mente, alma

prosseguiu por
"com"
seguido por "pra" ou "de"
mas poderoso o suficiente
ficar sozinho
como ele captura
pulmões, sangue, sonhos

o fim e o começo
permanecer
como se fosse recusar
desaparecimento
muito depois
a palavra está completa

persiste, permanece,
cresce
como se fosse substituir
o sujeito
que, por razões desconhecidas,
foi embora

fica macio no meu
palma
como se fosse preencher
as linhas de vida quebradas
pronunciado
por ter segurado com muita força

depois de aprender isso
palavra
seu ser permanece
com saudades,
como se fosse necessário
viver

The Same Meaning
(O Mesmo Significado)

There's a little girl,
Standing midway down the dark stairs,
Arms crossed and mouth pouted,
A crooked barrette in her blonde hair.
Her silence screaming: hear me.

There's a little girl,
Sneaking drinks out of bottles,
Backpack full but never used,
With her friends, skinny legs, running wild.
Her absence screaming: see me.

There's a little boy,
Every day, good as good can be,

Eyes and heart so open, valiantly,
Doing the right thing, never having a need.
His courtesy screaming: notice me.

There's a little boy,
Beautifully mischievous,
Rushing through the dishes, avoiding all his
chores,
Loving forbidden adventure, risks – even more.
His defiance screaming: accept me.
There are these men and women
Beautiful and worthy,
Standing frozen on their paths, shouting the
wrong words,
Running the wrong way,
Still, just longing: to be loved.

Can you help but wonder
How different they would plead
For words, for gifts, for love's embrace,
For all their wants and valid needs,
Had we just correctly heard: their screams.

***

Há uma menina,
Parado no meio das escadas escuras,
Braços cruzados e boca fazendo beicinho,
Uma presilha torta em seu cabelo loiro.

Silêncio dela gritando: me escute.

Há uma menina,
Tirando bebidas de garrafas,
Mochila cheia mas nunca usada
Com amigas, pernas magras, correndo solta.
Ausência dela gritando: me veja.

Há um garotinho,
Todos os dias, o melhor possível,
Olhos e coração tão abertos, bravamente,
Fazendo a coisa certa, sem precisar fazer isso.
Cortesia dele gritando: observe-me.

Há um garotinho,
Lindamente travesso,
Correndo pela louça, evitando todas as suas
tarefas,
Amando aventuras proibidas, riscos – ainda
mais.
Desafio dele gritando: me aceite.

Existem esses homens e mulheres
Lindão e dignão,
Parados congelados em seus caminhos, dizendo
as palavras erradas,
Correndo na direção errada,
Mesmo assim, só estão querendo: de ser amada.

É difícil não se perguntar
Quão diferente eles implorariam
Nas palavras, nos presentes, nos abraços
amorosos,
Para todos os seus desejos e necessidades
válidos,
Se ao menos tivéssemos ouvido corretamente:
seus gritos.

Take Flight

How can she admit
Her fear
Of cutting all ties
When the admission would make her weak?

How can she concede
Her desire
To have a string attached
When the concession would handcuff her?

How can she declare
Her conflict
About pushing him away
When the declaration would freeze her?

How can she disclose
Her tendency
To accept the unacceptable
When the disclosure would break her?

How can she profess
A love
That lives amongst such conflict
When the profession would expose her?

Weak, encaged,
Frozen and near broken,
She sees some freedom in such confessions:
Realizing, now, how could she not confess?

Temenos (Translating Love)

there, existed sharp needles, high walls of
brick and barbed-wire, a warrior
who stood diligent guard
around the area
bloody from
battle.

understand, i was speaking a language
that wasn't my own, hearing words
that were jumbled together by
forces and feelings distant
from royalty, from
romance.

so that place known as "temenos", meant
to be guarded as sacred, as special - i
confused with "ter medo" or "temer",
and, instead of giving tribute,
i guarded it with

fear.

understand, i didn't speak the languages:
not greek, not portuguese, not even
the english words that fell out of
my mouth but never matched
the words trapped in my
heart.

who knew? - not me - that this oasis
housing unpronounceable words
and unnamable jagged scars
was meant to be sacrosanct,
meant to be
revered.

and so, "com medo", i fought a losing
battle: to win the hearts of everyone,
including my very own, to translate
words of beauty and love, but
never lay eyes on the
blood.

but see, how very foolish, with such
mistaken guides: that very war-torn
scene had all the clues to construe
exactly where love lived
and breathed and
why.

the very place thought best avoided, was
the required destination, the brick and
barbed-wire a mistaken mirage,
where, existing all that time,
stood stained-glass and
candles.

not a wall to be defended, but within, an
altar to offer a piece of holy clothed
compassion, tender understanding;
to extend an eye as witness to
the pain of deep
wounds.

to follow the clues which seep from
the soil of these open sores
and find the words that
translate to healing,
to holding, to
love.

not to wash away the blood fearfully, but
to venerate, to cherish: the deepest
shades of its red color and its
path, lined by the elegant
sparkle of my veins,
majestic.

Scared, i could not translate love for anyone, let
alone myself. how magically different when
i unscrambled letters of the languages
i now speak: seeing me, my core,
my heart, my being, as
Sacred.

Moonlight

my sky blue sweatpants,
cozily shield my skin
from the cold sand,
covering my tan legs,
still firm but inches bigger
than that girl's,
three decades younger.

i sit here, a seat reserved for one,
silently watching the
water lap up against the
vast shoreline,
pretty relative to the streets
behind it, but without

the protection of a cove.

the soft sand, the water,
the paw prints, the chatter,
have space to spread out,
be near but far apart,
all framed by a setting sun
but missing the forced
intimacy of sloping cliffs.

my smile still gentle,
my face somehow melting
into its beauty with age,
the gentle creases plotting the
edges of big eyes not
committing any harsh crime
against that teenage girl.

no imagination is required
to see her disrobing her clothes,
sprinkling them onto a towel
as her tanned feet danced
through the rough sand toward
the water, the only language - laughter,
ready for the far-past-dusk swim.

one hundred miles and
thirty-three years carries
how many lifetimes and

moments that fade away,
and yet there she is, vibrant,
in a borrowed red swimsuit
looking over her right shoulder.

the waves much stronger then
than now, as if scrunched into
too little space, but there, inviting those two,
the calm right behind the break:
deeper, full of potential.
"will you keep me safe?",
still the coyest thing i ever said.

younger, but already having
learned languages she did not speak,
his reply, a simple, strong, penetrating "yes."
tonight, she can see clearly
herself in his eyes so many years ago -
golden, bronze, glistening;
his gaze, holding only her, spoke all the rest.

the sun is shimmering on water now,
as the moonlight was then;
that near midnight swim, she had walked
right into the sparkling trail of salt water,
unmoored by not one thing, by nothing,
caught in his pure celebration
of her presence.

that the water was cold,
the coved beach dark
but for the light of the moon,
that they would kiss under
water and by the swell,
and need to navigate back to shore,
all distant thoughts then, now the closest
memories.

that very moment
likely not even a full minute,
so fleeting before he held her hand
to dive under the first crashing
wave, them capably leading
each other to that gentle swell,
just behind the transforming line of the wave
break.

in her 50 years it is those
50 seconds that speak to
her a language with words
she searches for, passionately, now:
the light of his eyes and the moon
surrounding her with letters
that spelled everything and anything.

if i walked into this
cold pacific water tonight,
straight into the path playing

with the glitter of a distant summer sun,
i would still be that girl
who, for one minute, knew
the many things love could be.

the most miraculous
piece of this peaceful memory,
so powerful throughout the gentle years of
Moonlight,
still expanding my vision of what could be:
that even without having love's vocabulary,
she asked for safety
and trusted his answer.